917.97
STR

Strudwick, Leslie
Washington
34880000823190

WASHINGTON

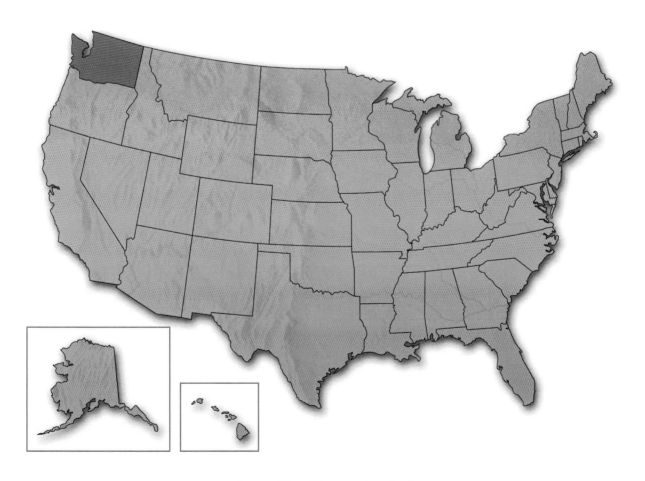

Leslie Strudwick

Published by Weigl Publishers Inc.
123 South Broad Street, Box 227
Mankato, MN   56002
USA
Web site: http://www.weigl.com
Copyright © 2001 WEIGL PUBLISHERS INC.
All rights reserved. No part of this publication may be reproduced,
stored in a retrieval system, or transmitted in any form or by any
means, electronic, mechanical, photocopying, recording, or otherwise,
without the prior written permission of Weigl Publishers Inc.

Library of Congress Cataloging-in-Publication Data available upon
request from the publisher. Fax: (507) 388-2746 for the attention of the
Publishing Records Department.

ISBN 1-930954-95-6

Printed in the United States of America
1 2 3 4 5 6 7 8 9 10   05 04 03 02 01

Project Coordinators
Rennay Craats
Jennifer Nault
Substantive Editor
Carlotta Lemieux
Copy Editors
Heather Kissock
Michael Lowry
Designers
Warren Clark
Terry Paulhus
Photo Researcher
Michael Lowry

Photograph Credits
Every reasonable effort has been made to trace ownership and to obtain
permission to reprint copyright material. The publishers would be
pleased to have any errors or omissions brought to their attention so
that they may be corrected in subsequent printings.

Cover: Corel Corporation; Bellingham/Whatcom County Convention & Visitors
Bureau: pages 3, (Bert Sagara) 4, 8 (Tore Ofteness), 11 (Keith Lazelle), 12, 15 (Jon
Brunk), 20 (Sally Moore), 22 (Norm McBeath), 23 (Douglas Wilson), 24 (Bert Sagara);
Used with the permission of Boeing Management Company: page 13; Corbis
Corporation: page 21, 26; © Corbis/Magma: page 6 (Neal Preston); Corel
Corporation: pages 10, 11, 13, 22, 23, 27; DGC Records: pages 3, 29 (Chris Cuffaro);
Digital Stock Corporation: page 14; Digital Vision Ltd: page 9, 21; Globe Photos Inc:
pages 6 (Romuald Meigneux), 24 (Walter Iooss Jr.), 26, 29 (John Barrett); Seattle King
County News Bureau: pages 5 & 12 (Nick Gunderson); Inns at Friday Harbor: pages
11, 20; Chihuly Studio: page 25 (Russell Johnson); Seattle Art Museum: page 24 (Paul
Macapia); North West Folk Life: pages 22, 25 (Bruce Milne); Minnesota Historical
Society: page 17, 18; Mississippi Tourism: page 20; Courtesy of National Park Service:
page 8, 10; Photodisk Corporation: page 27; Reuters/Archive Photos: pages 13
(Anthony Bolante), 26 (Joe Giza), 27 (Asusumu Takahashi); Monique de St. Croix:
page 15; W. Lynn Seldon Jr.: page 28; Starbucks Coffee International: page 14;
Steinhart, Jim of www.planetware.com: page 12; Tri-Cities Visitor & Convention
Bureau: pages 3, 4, 9, 17, & 22 (Stephen Kingsford Smith); U.S. Bureau of
Reclamation: pages 5, 28; U.S. Geologic Survey: page 7; USDA Forest Service: page 7
(J. Hughes); S. Vento: pages 15, 21; Visuals Unlimited: page 6 (Inga Spence);
Washington Apple Commission: page 14; Washington State Historical Society,
Tacoma: pages 4, 16, 17, 18, 19.

CONTENTS

INTRODUCTION

Although it is known as the Evergreen State, Washington has far more to offer than its trees. There are many lakes, towering mountains, and diverse natural regions. Along with Oregon, Idaho, and Alaska, Washington is part of the United States' Pacific Northwest region. This group of states has rugged landscapes, friendly people, a rich Native American heritage, and great scenery.

QUICK FACTS

As well as the Evergreen State, Washington is sometimes called the Chinook State.

The state motto is "Alki." It is a Chinook word meaning "by and by." The settlers called Alki Point "New York Alki," hoping the area would become the New York of the west coast "by and by."

Washington's Native Americans celebrate their culture during the Columbia River Salmon Powwow.

The ferry is a popular form of transportation for tourists visiting the San Juan Islands.

Getting There

Washington is bordered by Oregon to the south and Idaho to the east. The Pacific Ocean lies to the west, and Canada is directly north. Visitors can get to Washington by many forms of transport. Most airlines fly into both of the state's main airports: Seattle-Tacoma International and Spokane International. An abundance of highways and roads take people to all corners of the state and beyond. By train, visitors can enter Washington from the north, south, or east. When coming from the west, travelers will likely be on one of Washington's many ferries.

Washington's most important river, the Columbia River, provides a waterway for large, oceangoing vessels. The Columbia River enters Washington from the north and flows westward to the Pacific Ocean. It is the second longest river in the Western Hemisphere that flows into the Pacific Ocean.

QUICK FACTS

Dark green is the background for the state flag. The state seal is in the center.

Washington is the only state named after an American president.

The Grand Coulee Dam, built on the Columbia River, is the largest concrete dam in the United States.

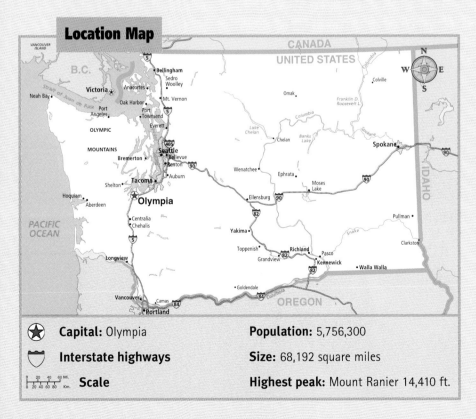

Location Map

★ **Capital:** Olympia

🛡 **Interstate highways**

Scale
0 20 40 60 MI.
0 20 40 60 80 Km.

Population: 5,756,300

Size: 68,192 square miles

Highest peak: Mount Ranier 14,410 ft.

Washington is well recognized for its beautiful scenery and wildlife. However, the people of the state also contribute to its popularity. Microsoft founder Bill Gates, who is the richest person in the world, has put Seattle on the map as a center for high-technology. In the 1990s, Seattle was also a trendsetter in the music industry. Many **grunge** bands were formed, following the lead of Seattle bands such as Nirvana and Pearl Jam.

Pearl Jam's first album, *Ten*, was a multimillion-seller.

Bill Gates was born on October 28, 1955. He grew up in Seattle.

QUICK FACTS

Helen Davis wrote the words and music of "Washington, My Home." It became the state song in 1959.

The square dance was chosen as Washington's state dance in 1979.

SMP

Another famous name in Washington is Mount Saint Helens. In May 1980, this volcano erupted for the first time in 123 years. The eruption sent ash 15 miles up into the air. Many towns were blanketed by inches of volcanic ash. Airborne ash covered 22,000 square miles, and could be seen in the air as far away as Montana. Mount Saint Helens has remained quiet ever since. In May 2000, there was renewed interest in the volcano when Washingtonians celebrated the twentieth anniversary of the eruption.

QUICK FACTS

The area of Washington is 68,192 square miles. It is the eighteenth largest state.

Geologists predict that Mount Saint Helens will erupt again in the future.

Ten million trees were blown down during the eruption of Mount Saint Helens.

The eruption of Mount Saint Helens gave geologists a chance to study a volcano in action.

The top of Mount Saint Helens is now a horseshoe-shaped crater with a rim reaching elevations of about 8,000 feet.

Puget Sound is a deep inlet that stretches 100 miles.

LAND AND CLIMATE

The Coast Ranges run along the western part of Washington. Most people live in the Puget Sound Lowlands, a valley running from Canada south to Oregon. Scattered around upper Puget Sound are the San Juan Islands, an **archipelago** of 172 islands.

More mountains border the lowlands on the east. The Cascade Mountains run from north to south, and the Rocky Mountains lie in the northeast corner. Many of the mountains in the Cascades were once active volcanoes.

The climate in Washington is greatly influenced by the Cascade Mountains. West of the Cascades, winters are mild and summers are warm. Rain falls throughout the year, with snow falling mainly near the mountains. On the eastern side of the Cascades, summers are hot and dry. However, winters are cold and snow is common. Average rainfall is 6 inches per year in the eastern part of the state, while it is over 60 inches per year near the west coast.

NATURAL RESOURCES

Washington is rich in natural resources. The most important resources are lumber, water, and fish. Today, there is much debate in the state over the use of these resources. Over the decades, industries have cut down forests, fished the waters, and drained rivers to **irrigate** fields. Industries were beginning to **deplete** the state's natural resouces. Once people realized the impact these industries were having on the environment, measures were taken to protect it. Many industries continue to use the state's natural resources, but **environmentalists** have been working hard to control the level of harm to the environment. Washington still has beautiful forests, rich soil, many rivers and lakes, and abundant wildlife.

The ground also holds rich resources. Gold, clay, peat, **olivine**, and limestone are all mined in Washington. Among the state's mined products, sand and gravel are the most highly valued. Both are used in construction.

Irrigation is a common practice for farmers who need more water than is naturally available.

QUICK FACTS

There are three National Parks and two National Historic Parks in Washington.

The Washington state gem is petrified wood.

In the past, Washington's forests have been clear-cut by the timber industry, leaving ugly, bare patches of land.

PLANTS AND ANIMALS

Trees cover much of the western part of Washington. Western hemlock and Douglas fir are most **plentiful** at the lower elevations. Higher up on the mountains, mountain hemlock and Pacific silver fir cover the land.

It is impossible to observe Washington's plant life without considering the state's ancient rain forest. Washington's Olympic Peninsula has some of the world's largest trees, including Sitka spruce, western red cedar, Douglas fir, and western hemlock. Most of them are about 200 feet high, but some trees grow as high as 300 feet. The ground and most of the trees are covered in moss, which thrives in areas of high rainfall.

Eastern Washington has far fewer trees. In the more northern mountains, there are ponderosa pines. The southern farmland area is dominated by prairie **vegetation** such as sagebrush.

The trees in the Olympic rain forest have never been logged. In fact, there are even some areas in the Olympic Mountains that have never been explored.

QUICK FACTS

More than 3,000 kinds of wildflowers grow in Washington.

The state flower is the western rhododendron. It is also called the coast and pink rhododendron.

The state tree is the western hemlock. It is also known as the Pacific hemlock, the hemlock spruce, Prince Albert's fir, and the Alaskan pine.

Wild animals roam the entire state. From mountain lions to mountain goats and from elk to coyotes, the state has plenty of wildlife. It is especially plentiful in the sky. Washington is known as a bird watcher's paradise. One of the most notable and common sights is the bald eagle.

Thousands of these eagles spend the winter just north of Seattle on the Skagit River. They share the sky with hundreds of other bird species, including owls, hawks, and smaller birds such as robins and finches.

The water is also rich in wildlife. Salmon swim in the state's many rivers. Crabs, lobsters, oysters, and clams share the coastal waters with killer whales and gray whales. Boat trips are available for those interested in seeing these huge mammals swim, feed, and play in the ocean.

Killer whales are a popular attraction along the Washington coast. They are related to dolphins and travel in groups called pods.

QUICK FACTS

Washington is home to many **endangered** animals, including the peregrine falcon, grizzly bear, gray wolf, and Columbian white-tailed deer.

The state bird is the willow goldfinch.

Washington is known for its salmon fishing, but the steelhead trout is the state fish.

TOURISM

Tourism is a growing industry in Washington. With so many state and national parks, Washington has an array of natural areas where people can hike, camp, ski, bike, fish, and boat. Hiking is popular with visitors and residents alike. Dozens of books have been written about Washington's superb hiking trails.

One popular tourist spot is Mount Saint Helens. Residents within the community have tried to make the best of the disaster by selling items made from the mountain's volcanic ash. Also, tourists can hire a helicopter or plane to fly over the volcano and look down into the crater.

Seattle, Washington's largest city, attracts many visitors. Seattle is a world-class port city with many museums, restaurants, festivals, and sports teams.

QUICK FACTS

The Space Needle is one of Seattle's most famous landmarks. It was built for the 1962 World's Fair. It stands 605 feet high.

In 1962, the first monorail in the United States was built in Seattle for the World's Fair.

The Space Needle has a revolving restaurant that completes a full turn every hour.

Along with its Seattle headquarters, Boeing has workers in more than sixty countries.

INDUSTRY

The **aerospace industry** is one of the largest in the state. The Boeing Company has its official headquarters in Seattle, and its final assembly plant is located in Everett. In fact, the plant is the world's largest building. William Boeing started the company in 1916. It built planes to fight in both world wars. The Boeing Company then turned its focus toward **commercial** jets. Today, Boeing is the largest employer in the state, and the Seattle plant employs more people than any other business in the city.

Another industry that has grown over the years is the electronics and computer software industry. Microsoft began in Seattle. It is now the leading software-producing company in the nation. Washington's other major industries include shipping, food processing, logging, fishing, and agriculture.

QUICK FACTS

Seattle is the second largest **container port** in the United States.

Many of the products and much of the food processed in Washington are sent to Asian countries such as Japan.

One-third of the timber cut each year in Washington is turned into pulp and made into paper.

About 24 percent of Washington's labor force work in the industry sector.

The Microsoft Corporation is one of the most successful companies in the United States. The name Microsoft is a combination of the words "microcomputer" and "software."

GOODS AND SERVICES

Washington's fertile soil is responsible for its strong agriculture industry. The state produces a wide range of fruit and vegetables. Washington's fresh produce is distributed across the state and all over the world. Three of Washington's biggest crops are apples, potatoes, and wheat. Washington grows more apples than any other state, with over 10 billion harvested in some years. The state's specialty is red delicious.

When rainfall is scarce, irrigation supplies crops with much needed water.

QUICK FACTS

Washington leads the nation in trade with Asia.

About 50,000 people are hired every summer to pick the state's apples.

The famous Starbucks Coffee Company is based in Seattle.

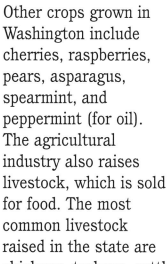

Other crops grown in Washington include cherries, raspberries, pears, asparagus, spearmint, and peppermint (for oil). The agricultural industry also raises livestock, which is sold for food. The most common livestock raised in the state are chickens, turkeys, cattle, swine, and sheep.

Although Washington farmers grow a lot of food, only about 4 percent of the population work in the agricultural industry. Far more people, about 29 percent, work in the service industry. Many work as computer programmers or in the restaurant trade. Another 22 percent are employed in wholesale or retail trade. Only about 12 percent of Washingtonians work in manufacturing.

Seafood lovers come from around the world to sample Washington's fresh fish.

The Makah attached sealskin balloons to their whale harpoons to prevent pierced whales from diving and swimming away.

FIRST NATIONS

Before Washington became a state, many different Native Peoples lived in the area. Their living conditions and what they ate depended on where they lived. The coastal groups included the Makah, Quinault, Duwamish, Skokomish, Skagit, Nooksack, Snoqualmie, and Snohomish. They obtained much of their food from the sea—they were skilled fishers and hunters of seals and whales. Their homes and boats were built from huge cedar trees that grew in the area.

East of the Cascade Mountains were the Okanagan, Colville, Spokane, Yakama, Nez Percé, and Palouse. These groups had to travel further in their search for food. They hunted rabbit, deer, and elk, and caught salmon. They made their homes out of grass or branches placed over large pits. These deep pithouses protected them from the wind and the cold.

The Chinook were a link between the eastern and western groups. They lived along the Columbia River and were mostly traders. The Chinook traded items between the eastern and western groups.

After a whale hunt, meat and blubber were divided up according to tribal customs.

George Vancouver spent three years
exploring North America's west coast.

EXPLORERS

The first Europeans to the present-day state of
Washington came in the late 1700s. Spanish and
British explorers stopped along the Washington coast
to trade with Native Americans and gather furs.
Explorers such as James Cook and George Vancouver
named many places along the coast.

The first explorers arrived by sea in 1780. They
were fur traders. One of them was Robert Gray,
captain of the *Columbia*. In 1792, Gray sailed into the
mouth of a great river, which he named after his ship.
After Gray's trip, the United States claimed the region.
President Thomas Jefferson heard about the money
being made in the fur trade. He sent two army officers,
William Clark and Meriwether Lewis, to explore and map the
route from the Mississippi River to the Pacific Ocean. This
new route allowed traders and settlers to travel to the
west by land as well as by sea.

QUICK FACTS

After Lewis and Clark's
trip, the area west of
the Rocky Mountains
became known as the
Oregon Territory.

The Columbia River is
the second longest river
in the United States.

The Lewis and Clark
Expedition set off in May,
1804, and arrived home
in September, 1806. They
covered a total of about
8000 miles, from a camp
outside St. Louis to the
Pacific Ocean and back.

Meriwether   William
Lewis   Clark

Marcus Whitman helped bring settlers to the Pacific Northwest.

MISSIONARIES

Along with traders came early missionaries. They came to teach **Christianity** to the Native Peoples. Two early missionaries were Marcus and Narcissa Whitman. They lived in peace with the Cayuse until 1847, when an epidemic of measles struck the people in the area. Although the Whitmans helped care for the sick, most of the European children lived, while about half of the Cayuse, including almost all of the children, died. The chief ordered the Whitmans and some other settlers to be killed. They killed fourteen people and burnt down the mission buildings. Native Peoples continued to die from diseases, starvation, and poor living conditions.

QUICK FACTS

The large Oregon Territory was divided into the smaller territories of Oregon and Washington in 1853.

The Whitman mission has been turned into a National Historical Site.

Many Native Peoples accepted the Christian faith in exchange for food and shelter at missions.

Some of Washington's older trees are over ten feet wide.

EARLY SETTLERS

The first settlers to Seattle came west for the fur trade. Fort Vancouver and Spokane House were among the first fur-trading posts.

After the United States claimed the territory, the government offered free land to any settler willing to live and work on it. In the mid-1800s, people began to move to the area in large numbers. Lumberjacks and loggers were quick to set up sawmills. The trees in Washington were some of the biggest they had ever seen. It was not long before towns and cities emerged around the sawmills.

In 1883, the Northern Pacific Railway was complete. It was now easier to travel to the west coast. The natural resources were so plentiful that people continued to pour into the area. In order to move raw materials to other regions, shipbuilding and shipping industries grew quickly.

QUICK FACTS

The settlers who named Seattle did so in honor of a Squamish chief.

By 1889, Washington Territory had more than 300,000 residents.

In the late 1800s, the logging industry employed two-thirds of the people in the state.

Since the mid-1800s, Washington's timber industry has played an important role in the state's economy.

POPULATION

Washington is home to more than 5.7 million people. Most are of European descent. African Americans are the next largest cultural group. Hispanics, Asians, Pacific Islanders, and Native Americans make up the rest of the population.

Almost 75 percent of all the people in Washington live in Puget Sound. Washington's largest city, Seattle, is in this area, as well as the state capital, Olympia.

More than 500,000 people live in Seattle. The second largest city is Spokane, and Tacoma is the third largest city. Both have just under 200,000 people. In recent years, some Washingtonians have moved away from the big cities. They are choosing to live a more relaxed lifestyle in the countryside or on the San Juan Islands.

QUICK FACTS

About 104,000 Native Americans still live in Washington. This is less than 2 percent of the state's population.

In 1890, there were about 357,000 people living in Washington.

There are about 5,756,300 people living in the state.

Many people attend Washington's music festivals.

POLITICS AND GOVERNMENT

The government of Washington is centered in Olympia, the capital. There are three branches of government in the state. The first is the executive. This branch decides how the state's money will be spent. It also ensures that laws made by the state are carried out. The governor, who is elected to a four-year term, is head of this branch. The lieutenant governor, secretary of state, attorney general, and treasurer make up the executive branch under the governor.

The second branch is the legislative branch. This branch makes the laws of the state. It consists of the Senate and the House of Representatives.

The judicial branch consists of all the courts of the state. These include local courts as well as the Supreme Court. This branch ensures that citizens of the state obey the laws.

QUICK FACTS

There are forty-nine members in the State Senate.

Ninety-eight members make up Washington's House of Representatives.

Washington became a state in 1889.

The biggest political debates in Washington are over the environment and natural resources.

The State Capitol in Olympia resembles the nation's Capitol in Washington, D.C.

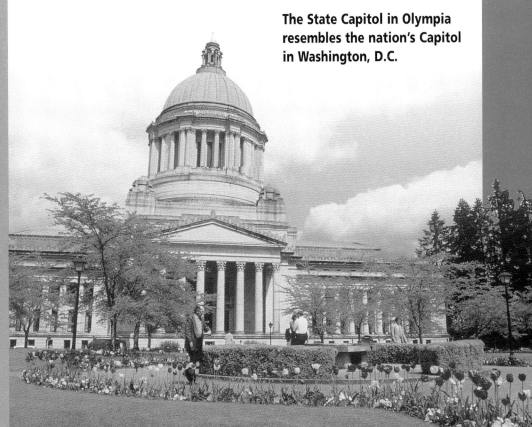

CULTURAL GROUPS

Although their numbers are small, Native Americans add much to the culture of Washington. Some Native Americans in the area lost touch with their early traditions when settlers arrived, forcing them to move to reservations. Today, they are trying to bring all parts of their culture back to life. For instance, Native Peoples along the Washington coast are well known for their beautiful and colorful totem poles, which they carve in the traditional style. Also, the Museum of Native American Culture in Spokane displays items and artifacts that represent the strong cultures that once flourished in the area.

QUICK FACTS

Most of Washington's minority groups, except for Native Americans, live in the bigger cities.

People of Scandinavian descent in Poulsbo celebrate a Viking Festival each May. It includes a parade and Norwegian food and entertainment.

Many African Americans and Hispanics came to Washington during World War II to find work.

Many cultural celebrations in Washington showcase Native Americans' cultural richness.

Many of Washington's early settlers came from England, Germany, and Scandinavia. Scandinavia includes Norway, Sweden, and Denmark, and sometimes Finland and Iceland. There are many people of Scandinavian descent living in Seattle. Many live in a district known as Ballard. Throughout Ballard, there are many Scandinavian features. For example, Ballard has a large, historical mural that was donated by the King and Queen of Norway in 1996.

There has been a large Asian population in the state since its early days. In the 1800s, Japanese and Chinese workers helped build the railroad. They also planted orchards and fished in the area. More Asian people have been moving to the state in recent decades. Many come from Vietnam, the Philippines, Korea, and Thailand.

QUICK FACTS

The whole town of Leavenworth has been rebuilt to look like a traditional German village.

The German community of Leavenworth holds a festival each fall called Oktoberfest.

Seattle's Chinese community celebrates its culture throughout the year, including the Chinese Culture and Arts Festival held in June.

ARTS AND ENTERTAINMENT

Much like other states of the Pacific Northwest, there is plenty to do in Washington's great outdoors. Hiking, skiing, snowboarding, kayaking, rock climbing, biking, and surfing are especially popular.

For those who prefer the arts, the state offers both indoor and outdoor arts venues. Seattle is the biggest cultural center in Washington. It has some of the state's top museums, including the Seattle Art Museum and the Pacific Science Center. Seattle also hosts a yearly arts festival called Bumbershoot. The Bumbershoot festival takes place during the Labor Day weekend and features dance, theater, and comedy shows.

QUICK FACTS

The famous guitar player and rock singer of the 1960s and 1970s, Jimi Hendrix, was from Seattle.

Bing Crosby, the singer and actor who sang "White Christmas," grew up in Spokane. There is now a Crosby Student Center at Gonzaga University.

In 1974, Spokane hosted a World's Fair. It was the smallest city ever to do so.

The Seattle Art Museum has a park on the waterfront featuring outdoor sculpture.

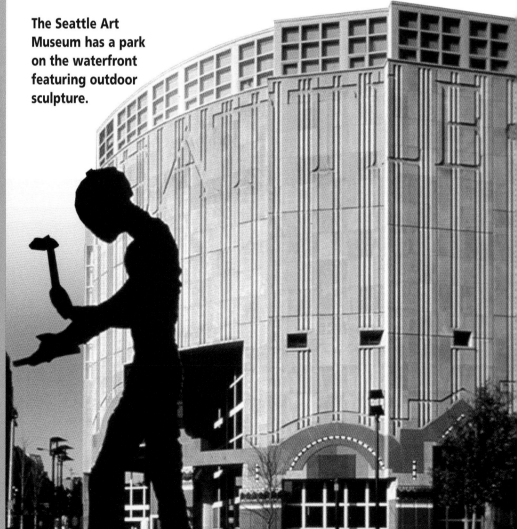

The Northwest Folklife Festival in Seattle features many interesting and colorfully costumed people.

Hardly a month goes by in Washington when there is not a festival of some kind. Music, sports, and international festivals highlight different aspects of the state. The Washington International State Fair takes place in Everett once a year. As well, there is a Rodeo Days Festival in Cheney and a June Blues Festival and Workshop in Port Townsend.

Arts and crafts fairs can be found across the state throughout the year. Native Americans still practice many of their traditional arts and crafts. Crafts such as beadworking, carving, and basket making are very popular. The Northwest Arts and Crafts Fair held in Seattle is one of the largest in the state.

QUICK FACTS

The cartoonist who created "The Far Side" is Gary Larson. He grew up in Tacoma and now lives in Seattle.

Washington's Dale Chihuly became interested in glass while studying at the University of Washington. Today, he is known around the world for his glass creative sculptures. In 2001, a museum is scheduled to open in Tacoma, Chihuly's home town.

Dale Chihuly's glass art has been shown in over 180 museum collections.

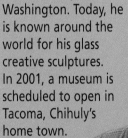

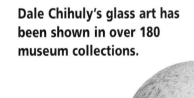

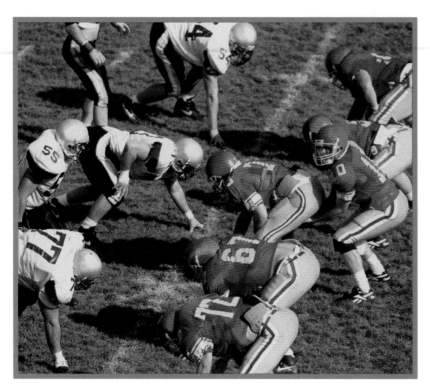

SPORTS

Sports are an important form of entertainment in Washington. If people are not taking part in a sport themselves, they will likely be watching the state's professional teams. Washington's three professional sports teams are all based in Seattle.

The Seattle Seahawks are members of the National Football League. Until recently, they shared their home field, the Kingdome, with the state's baseball team, the Seattle Mariners. In 1999, the Mariners built a new home—Safeco Field. This modern stadium has real grass and a **retractable** roof. In 2000, the old and less popular Kingdome was torn down. The Seahawks are playing at the University of Washington until their field is built. The new stadium will be where the Kingdome was, and it will host football and soccer games.

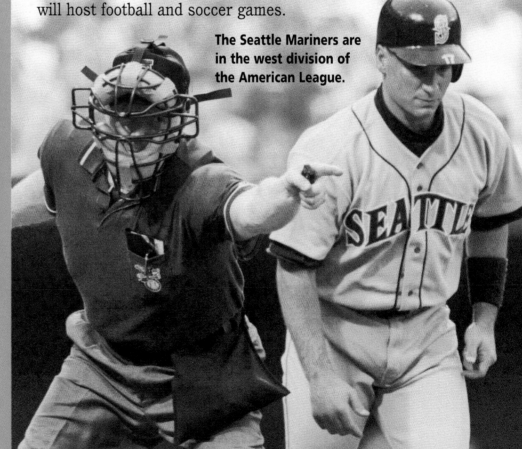

The Seattle Mariners are in the west division of the American League.

QUICK FACTS

Ken Griffey Sr. and Jr. made history in American baseball. They were the first father and son to be teammates—both played for the Seattle Mariners.

Ken Griffey Jr.

The Seattle Thunderbirds are the city's minor league hockey team. They share the Key Arena with the Supersonics.

In the National Basketball Association, Seattle is represented by the Supersonics. Fans pack the Key Arena whenever the team plays at home.

College-level sports are also popular across the state. Football is big on the University of Washington campus. The Huskies won the Rose Bowl six times between 1960 and 1992. The university also claims medals for rowing. The women's team won the Collegiate Varsity Eights Championship seven times during the 1980s. The men's team won in 1984.

The Seattle Supersonics joined the NBA for the 1967-69 season and won the NBA championship in the 1978-79 season.

QUICK FACTS

Washington has many world class golf courses. The state's natural diversity allows golfers an impressive choice of golf styles and conditions.

The Seattle International Raceway hosts car and motorcycle races throughout the year.

Brain Teasers

1 Washington is covered with parkland. How much land do state-run parks occupy?

Answer: About 255,000 acres of land are reserved for state parks.

2 Who helped the famed explorers Lewis and Clark?

Answer: A Native American woman from the Shoshone tribe called Sacagawea helped guide the men along their expedition.

3 How long did it take to build the Grand Coulee Dam?

Answer: It took eight years to complete the dam.

4 What is a young salmon called?

Answer: A young salmon is called a smolt.

5

What famous football quarterback is from Washington?

Answer: John Elway is from Port Angeles.

6

Make a guess: What is Bill Gates's full name?

Answer: His full name is William Henry Gates III.

7

What warning signs were there that Mount Saint Helens was about to erupt in 1980?

Answer: Mount Saint Helens did not suddenly erupt without warning. Although the huge eruption occurred in the middle of May, there were warning signs months earlier. The volcano began to rumble on March 20, 1980. Ten days later, steam started to rise from two new craters. These craters merged together in early April. The new crater measured about 1,700 feet across. Nearly seven weeks of minor earthquakes led to the eruption on May 18. The blast took 1,312 feet off the top of the volcano.

8

What Seattle rock band is given credit for creating grunge music?

Answer: Nirvana

FOR MORE INFORMATION

Books

Aylesworth, Thomas and Virginia.
Discovering America: The Northwest.
Chelsea House Publishers, 1996.

Bock, Judy, and Rachel Kranz.
Scholastic Encyclopedia of the United States.
New York: Scholastic, 1997.

Pitcher, Don. *Washington Handbook.*
California: Moon Travel Handbooks, 1999.

Stefoff, Rebecca. *Celebrate the States:
Washington*. New York: Benchmark Books,
1999.

Web sites

You can also go online and have a look
at the following Web sites:

Access Washington
http://access.wa.gov

Washington State Tourism
http://www.tourism.wa.gov

Fact Monster
http://www.factmonster.com/ipka/A01082
86.html

Washington State History
http://www.theus50.com/washington

Some Web sites stay current longer than
others. To find other Washington Web
sites, enter search terms such as
"Washington," "Seattle," "Mount Saint
Helens," or any other topic you want
to research.

GLOSSARY

aerospace industry: the industry of designing, building, and operating aircraft

archipelago: a chain of islands

Christianity: a religion which believes that Jesus Christ lived and was the son of God

commercial: for profit; to make money

container port: a shipping port for very large cargo or containers

deplete: to decrease a supply or resource

endangered: in danger of becoming extinct

environmentalist: a person who works to protect Earth, including the environment, plants, and animals

grunge: alternative rock music from the early 1990s

irrigate: to supply land or crops with water by means of a ditch, pipe, or stream

olivine: any member of a group of common magnesium minerals

plentiful: abundant; many

reservations: areas of land set aside for Native Americans

retractable: having the ability to draw back in

vegetation: plant life

INDEX